AMERICA'S 25 ISSUES TO FIX AND MAKE THE UNITED STATES GREAT, AGAIN!

Peter D. Fleming

authorHOUSE®

AuthorHouse™
1663 Liberty Drive
Bloomington, IN 47403
www.authorhouse.com
Phone: 1-800-839-8640

First published by AuthorHouse 7/25/2011

ISBN: 978-1-4490-5055-9 (e)
ISBN: 978-1-4490-5053-5 (sc)
ISBN: 978-1-4490-5054-2 (hc)

Library of Congress Control Number: 2009913466

Printed in the United States of America

This book is printed on acid-free paper.

Proceeds from the sale of this book
will go to support Truelander Dreams.
A Veteran run organization, helping Veterans...
www.truelanderdreams.com

Section I

It is ok to be proud to be an American,
even if we need to find it's not perfect...

"Look back over the past, with its changing empires that
rose and fell, and you can foresee the future, too."

- <u>Marcus Aurelius</u>-

"We stand today at a crossroads: One path
leads to despair and utter hopelessness. The
other leads to total extinction. Let us hope we
have the wisdom to make the right choice."

-<u>Woody Allen</u>-

Opening thoughts...

Do you enjoy your freedoms and rights? Well of course you do. We have the choice of any type of music, movies, the freedom of movement, expression, to bear arms, live free as we wish. We have a Constitution that provides us with the written proof of these rights and freedoms. That is what made this country so great.

The United States of America was once considered the greatest example of what a nation should be. We were viewed as the example of what a person could do, if he/she had the willingness to try. All they had to do was have a dream, drive, and a willingness to follow through. People from all walks of life came here to follow their dreams. In a very short time we went from a mismatched group of colonies to a nation the world both feared and respected.

To understand ourselves we must try to understand the world in which we live. Our political state has become deeply intertwined with the rest of the world. Our political and economic influence has reached every corner of the globe. Some of this has been intentional and some by chance. By intentional, I mean that our government has actively gotten involved in the affairs of foreign nations (Kosovo, Vietnam, Taiwan...) and by chance is more the influence of our 'pop-culture' (movies, music, magazines...)

Currently there are 203 sovereign 'nation states'. These are then split into two groups, 193 which are sovereign, to include those with membership in the United Nations and the remainder have 'de facto' or 'de jure' status, but are not universally recognized by other nations. Keep in mind this may not be completely accurate due to the fluidity of the 'nation building process', wars, coups, and other such activities.

Politics have now become a part of everyday activities. Trade negotiations are dictated on commerce and trade, which is nothing new. What has changed is the depth to which these seemingly unconnected events are intertwined. A hundred years ago it was common for entire communities to be almost entirely self-sufficient. But that has changed which each passing generation.

We now rely on products not just from neighboring communities or even neighboring states but from foreign nations. Whether it is clothing from China or tech support from India we have reached a point that we now rely very heavily on foreign products and services. This fact is then exploited during trade negotiations.

The United States was once an industrialized nation but we have become a service oriented society. We continually rely on outside sources to provide our needs, our products and our services. This has greatly weakened our nation. We have reached a point where we really don't have anything to offer our trade partners. Though we live in a nation rich in resources, we lack the productivity needed to recreate products sought by foreign markets.

It takes less time to slide backwards than it does to move forward. The US has been sliding the wrong direction for some time now. However, it is not too late to stop, regroup, pick up the pieces, and move forward again. We just have a series of issues which needed to be addressed, properly dissected, and actively corrected.

Because somehow, in the last fifty to sixty years, the United States went from being the strongest nation on the planet to being viewed as the cause of all the world's problems. How far the mighty can fall, we were the winners of World War Two, defenders of freedom and free enterprise, and are now viewed as the primary cause of the global financial crisis and evil war mongers. Well that is simply not the case.

Everyone likes to point fingers as to who is to blame for our current predicament. The east blames the west, democrats blame the republicans, the poor blame the rich, the liberals blame the conservatives, the religious blame the non-religious, the dogs blame the cats... and so it goes for the past couple of decades. All the while no one actually fixes the problem. Depending to which party is in power depends on which problem gets money thrown at it.

That is not a solution. Name calling, mudslinging, finger pointing, blame shifting, call it what you will, does not solve the issues. We need to get past the 'who' caused the major issues, because the reality is in a democratic re-public, which the United States is suppose to be, the fault lies with each and every citizen.

Now we need to focus on how to fix it, for the greater good of all. In a nation of 300,000,000 (three hundred million) plus people, compromises need to be made, concessions on both sides. That does not mean giving up your core beliefs. What that does mean is looking at the bigger picture. One needs to ask, what is in the best interest of America's future? The decisions made today may not have a huge impact of those living now but, what about the future generations?

The first place these various groups need to turn is to the US Constitution. The second place to turn for answers is within our own nation and our needs. Not the needs of our allies, not the needs of the rest of the world but home. We need to look within ourselves, our national needs, our Constitution.

That is what made this country so great. At one point people looked to the future. They came here with hopes and dreams, a desire to make something greater than themselves. Maybe only a small portion was fortunate enough to achieve such success but, that didn't stop millions from trying.

It is time to go back to the innovative, independent, free-spirited nation we once were. Somehow we went from proud, honorable, and head strong nation of go getters to an almost weak, ashamed, and codependent nation. There is too much reliance on the government to provide, protect, and run our lives.

It is time, actually past time, to return to our roots. There may be a lot of naysayers who think it is too late, and we have a planet full of those who would love to see this great nation collapse. But with a few changes and a return to a time of independent pride and a need to create self-worth we could be the envy of the world again.

It would only take a few simple changes. We need to drastically rethink the way we see not only the world but our government. We need to remember who runs our country, the politicians or those who voted and got them elected. It may seem overwhelming when one thinks of all the various issues that affect us in our daily lives. Actually it is quite simple. Just need to break it down into simple measurements.

Now What?

First you must realize I didn't just dream this stuff up. After years of talking and listening (something often forgotten) with other armchair intellects, it became painfully clear that the issues and problems of our country are on everyone's mind. All one needs to do is watch the news, read the headlines, or conduct a simple internet search and it will become very apparent just how many Americans feel this way.

There have been several polls conducted by the media, Readers Digest, Gallop polls, and by other sources they all seem to come to the same conclusion. America's top issues are related to healthcare, the overall economy, energy, tax, the war(s), terrorism, moral values, illegal immigration, and too much government just to name a few.

All one needs to do is read the major headlines of the daily papers, or that show up on your MSN or Yahoo home page and you will see. For those who are a bit more active, a quick search of the internet, blogs, and everyday people everywhere are all saying the same thing. America has some major issues. This is nothing new and not the rhetoric of talk shows and news radio this is a fact that needs to be dealt with before it gets anymore out of hand.

I come from a military background and have worked as a contractor. This has given me the unique perspective. Not only did it allow me to see the world, I saw the world through the eyes of foreign nationals and through the eyes of fellow Americans, actually a good sampling of America's population. I have listened to, talked with, and debated with people from Alabama to Washington State, and from Central America to Europe to the Middle East, all with their own perspective.

These people are all of various backgrounds, educations, religious beliefs, races, ages just a few from the spectrum of the people that represent all walks of life. They all have opinions, we all know the saying about opinions... But if you take a moment to realize that for all our differences there is a common thread.

The United States has problems (duh). The US butts into every other country's business, their politics, their social structures, their personal choices and tries to change them. I am not saying that I agree with the politics of these other countries. I am just saying maybe it is not our responsibility to effect change.

Especially when one considers all the issues we currently have in our own country. We are a nation that suffers from deep debt, sky-rocketing health care cost, loss of the middle class, deteriorating infrastructure, reverse in race relations, poor academics, loss of civil liberties, weak financial stability, and the list goes on. So until we fix these issues what gives us the right to dictate how any other nation should be run?

Furthermore, the solutions to any nation's problems begin with the citizens of that nation. They need to step up and demand the wanted changes. Not flee to another country, taking their social problems with them. They should create a place where they are happy to live in, just as our fore fathers did with the United States. They came together and formed a union of separate colonies into one strong nation. It was not easy but they knew what they wanted and made it happen.

Here in the United States we have reached a point where we need to take back our nation. To effect those promised changes, not just for the sake of change but, because our nation needs to find its center again. We have strayed way off course for far too long. So instead of trying to fix the world it is time we focus on ourselves. That does not mean we need to become an isolationist society just that we need to become a little more self focused. At least, we should look inward, until a time where our issues don't out-weigh the solutions.

What is listed here is a very brief to the point breakdown of the issues affecting the United States today. These are compiled from normal Americans who just have had enough of false promises and empty pledges. There are those who may see this as an oversimplified breakdown of our nation's issues. But we need to start somewhere.

Here is a basic outline of our nation's core issues, as seen through the eyes of both US citizens and foreigners. Now you may not agree with this list, you may think of others as being more important, that is fine. The intention of this is more as discussion points, food for thought, and a direction for future politics.

If we were able to fix just this small list of issues many of the other issues would automatically be resolved. There is a severe case of cause and effect, when one issue is allowed to go it feeds another which then feeds another. By that same token, when you correct a root issue the others will become non-existent or at least return to a manageable state.

So here in no special order are America's top issues:

Section II

25 issues America should fix...

"Experts and the educated elite have replaced what worked with what sounded good. Society was far more civilized before they took over our schools, prisons, welfare programs, police departments and courts. It's high time we ran these people out of our lives and went back to common sense."

-Walter E. Williams-

A typical vice of American politics is the avoidance of saying anything real on real issues.

-Theodore Roosevelt-

1.

Take Personal Responsibility

"Most people do not really want freedom, because freedom involves responsibility, and most people are frightened of responsibility."

-Sigmund Freud-

"You cannot escape the responsibility of tomorrow by evading it today."

-Abraham Lincoln-

It is not everyone else's fault that things have ended up the way they are. It is ours. The hard cold truth is that we are to blame for America's current problems, you and me. But we are not to blame for the issues occurring in all the other nations of the world. The sooner we accept that the quicker we can move forward and correct the mistakes of the past. Everything that is a current issue may have been created out of Depression era politics, or Cold War paranoia, or the sexual revolution, or, or, or... That doesn't matter, what does is that we now take responsibility and correct this turn of events before it becomes permanent.

It is not society's fault that we have crime, it is societies fault that we hamper law enforcement and don't properly punish criminals, therefore creating a deterrence. It is not the government's responsibility to ensure health care, to pay your rent, or send your kids to college. Again that is your responsibility (read your Constitution). America was not founded as a socialist nation. Every good nation needs some social programs, but America's greatness lies with its individual spirit and lack of direct governmental control.

The United States was founded on people taking responsibility for their destinies. When they traveled across the Atlantic, fought disease, the native inhabitants, nature... they didn't have insurance, dedicated health care providers, or any of that. They had the shear will needed to create a life here. They took personal responsibility for their lives and their actions to carve out a life not only for themselves but future generations as well.

2.

Remember something called the Constitution (and the Declaration of Independence).

"We the people are the rightful masters of both Congress and the courts, not to overthrow the Constitution but to overthrow the men who pervert the Constitution."

-Abraham Lincoln-

"The Declaration of Independence, the Constitution, the Civil War-when I really think about them they all seem about as likely as the parting of the Red Sea."

-Sarah Vowell-

Our founding fathers set up the guidelines for our then newly created society to successfully coexist. It took 13 independent colonies and formed a single unified nation of individual states. A nation which not only was created but, earned its right to exist, by the blood, sweat, and tears of that and previous generations.

The Constitution and the Declaration of Independence are more than old parchments, more than a governmental outline but, is in fact a contractual agreement which the government is bound to follow. It sets our rights and privileges as citizens of this nation. It doesn't matter if you are a natural born or naturalized citizen you are still given all those rights and freedoms. The Constitution needs to not only be taught in our schools it should be requirement for graduation.

We need to hold our courts/judicial system and our politicians accountable. They are the ones who must follow the Constitution and ensure that every law and every decision does not contradict or go against it. If they were held accountable to the Constitution and followed it, we would have fewer issues to contend with. After all, we as citizens are held to a set standard so perhaps it is time to remind those in office that they must abide by the same standard.

3.

Return to family values and roots.

"The strength of a nation derives from
the integrity of the home."

-Confucius-

"Years ago nobody was elected on the economic ticket.
It was either the education platform, or it was health
or it was other issues. It is only recently that economic
values have superseded every other human value."

-Anita Roddick-

This one has been overstated in the political arena and therefore has lost its real meaning. Contrary to popular belief it does not take a village to raise a child. It takes parents. Not TV, the internet, chat rooms, video games, virtual worlds/friends but, actual parents. Yes it is a reality that we must work, that doesn't mean we can't still have an interest in the daily lives of the children.

We need to remember it is not the schools responsibility to raise children, not the government, not the village but the parents. Whether by accident or choice, single parent, married or not it still takes the parents to actively participate in the child's growth and development. Studies constantly show that children perform better when the parents are active in their children's lives.

It doesn't take much. It should not be that difficult to sit down for at least one meal a day. To be there during homework/study time or interact with the child. Take time to teach your loved ones how to cook, catch a ball, sew, paint, something that involves actual interaction and builds a bond that later in life will help the child to properly deal with the world they are in. Instead of turning to gangs, violence, or some on-line predator, they should turn to you as the role model, knowing right from wrong.

4.

Stop saying sorry.

"It is better to be safe than sorry."

- American Proverb-

"If it weren't the problem of politics for me, it would be another. And yet, sometimes it's so difficult. And I feel sorry for myself. And then hate myself for this feeling of self-pity."

-Julie Nixon Eisenhower-

We need to stop regretting our greatness and stop apologizing for what we have done as a nation and start being proud of what we have accomplished. Embrace that we live in what was the envy of the world. Embrace that we have a great military. Embrace our freedoms. Embrace that we are better than those who oppose us. Their jealousy is the best form of flattery.

Every nation has the ability to achieve what we have if they so choose. Other nations have resources and hard working intelligent citizens. Perhaps the people of those nations should take it upon themselves to make something of their own country. Rise up and make a nation they can be proud of. We should not feel sorry for their lack of willingness to achieve greatness, especially since we have spent billions and billions in nation building efforts in other countries. Only to have them turn against us.

So from now on, we need to not be sorry for others hardships and feel bad for our greatness. Instead we need to build ourselves back up. Create a competitive spirit that made us great in the first place. It is one thing to see a starving child and feel bad, it is something completely different to feel bad for having been born some place better. If you wish to help the misfortunate, that is great but, not at the price of America's potential greatness. We have been selling our soul for far too long.

5.

Stop the nation building.

"I am just absolutely convinced that the best formula for giving us peace and preserving the American way of life is freedom, limited government, and minding our own business overseas."

-Ron Paul-

"There are a growing number of conservatives and Republicans who, while they support the president and support the war in Iraq, wonder how many of these nation-building wars we're going to engage in and what the parameters of that are."

-Lamar Alexander-

It doesn't work. We go to other countries with the best of intentions and a desire to help. We spend billions to help recreate someone else's nation into one that fits our image. Usually it is neither welcomed nor appreciated. Oh, sure the money is nice. The wealthy get wealthier and power hungry get fed (though never full). It usually doesn't take long for the citizens to expect their nation to look like the magazines and movies, where everything is good and the story almost always ends with a happy ending. When it becomes apparent that those are just fantasy, and that it takes time and hard work, they soon grow tired of our intervention.

We spend all this money overseas to build schools, hospitals, bridges, roads, create infrastructures, and train/equip their military. Only to be told it is not enough and that we are not welcomed in their newly created nation. In time these places often end up on the opposite side of the political scope and thus we feel the need to correct this point of view. We have a long list which includes Iran, Iraq, the Philippians, Panama, Afghanistan, and at least a dozen more.

If the people are content with their nation the way it is, then let's leave it as is. If the people are not content with the status quo in their nation, it is their responsibility to change it, not ours. Those billions, if not trillions, could have been much better spent rebuilding our schools, hospitals, bridges, roads... and why would we want a foreign military that is equal to ours?

6.

We are not the 'World Police'.

"How did we win the election in the year 2000? We talked about a humble foreign policy: No nation-building; don't police the world. That's conservative, it's Republican, it's pro-American - it follows the founding fathers. And, besides, it follows the Constitution."

-Ron Paul-

"We Americans have no commission from God to police the world."

-Benjamin Harrison-

There is a common misconception that we are obligated to go to every third world country and eliminate their corrupt governments. That our military is to be used to chase everything from drug dealers to pirates. Both NATO and the United Nations (UN) feel free to support various operations by popular vote but, then seem to fail in sending the personnel and finances needed to accomplish their set resolutions. This shortcoming then, somehow, becomes the responsibility of the United States...

If something or someone is a direct military threat to our Allies and we are requested to assist, by all means we should help. But it is not America's responsibility to police warlords in Africa or Columbian drug cartels. We should not be out chasing pirates or whatever, in international waters. There are already agencies working together in joint task forces for that. The financial side of things is another issue. We should not be sixty percent (60%) of NATO's budget. NATO has how many members? (28)

If something is a direct threat to the welfare of the United States, such as terrorism, then of course we should be involved. But if it is joint operation, then we should be in a support role and only support to the nation(s) involved. When other nations support us financially then perhaps we should invest more. If NATO or the UN wants our involvement, either they should pay or our share should be proportionate to the services rendered. Otherwise we should be paid for our services when assisting other nations.

7.

Laws, statutes, ordnances, regulations, and amendments.

"It is difficult to make our material condition better by the best law, but it is easy enough to ruin it by bad laws."

-Theodore Roosevelt-

"The only power any government has is the power to crack down on criminals. Well, when there aren't enough criminals, one makes them. One declares so many things to be a crime that it becomes impossible for men to live without breaking laws."

-Ayn Rand-

We all know that even within a free society there must be set rules, guidelines which will dictate, to the populace, what is acceptable and what is not (i.e. the Constitution), within the collective society. Rules are a necessary evil for peaceful coexistence. Our forefathers knew this to be true, even when they broke from the British crown.

However, just how many laws are needed? The United States Code currently fills 27 volumes, plus supplements and indexes. There are also hundreds of new federal laws passed every year (and have been since the beginning) which may not result in any change in the codified statutes in the US Code. There have been more than 20,000 statutes enacted since 1789. Instead of constantly creating new laws to circumvent a previous law, why not just enforce the laws that are already present? If something is wrong, harmful, or disruptive of course it needs to regulated and wrong doers punished. But just how many laws do we need? There are so many currently on the books that even the lawyers need a library to track them.

There needs to be a serious audit and review of the current laws, be it federal, state, or local. The elected officials need to be held accountable and the constitutionality of any law, statute, ordnance, regulation, amendment needs to be questioned. The greater good of the society needs to outweigh the special interest groups.

8.

Hold elected officials accountable

"Public officers are the servants and agents
of the people, to execute laws which the
people have made and within the limits of a
constitution which they have established."

-Steven Grover Cleveland-

"Citizen participation is a device whereby
public officials induce nonpublic individuals
to act in a way the officials desire."

-Daniel P. Moynihan-

We live in a democratic republic. Which simply means two things; the majority rules and the majority are represented by elected officials. It does not matter the level of government in question. Whoever is in a public position of power, was placed there by popular vote. They are paid by tax dollars. They are called public servants for a reason. The reason is simple, they work for us, they are put in seats of power to represent our needs.

They work for us. We put them in power to do our bidding. They need to vote in a manner which supports the opinions, desires, and beliefs of the community they serve. Everyone needs to be represented, of course, but the opinion of the majority is who he/she was elected to represent. That is clearly the focal point of all decisions, not lobbyist, special interest, but the greater good of the voting populace.

If there comes a time when the politicians forget who they work for and forget why they were elected then they need to be removed. Instead of allowing them to pursue their own agendas, while the voting public quietly sits by complaining about it. We need to voice our grievances and if we are not heard then we need to remove/impeach that official. Perhaps the next one will listen to who placed them in power in the first place.

9.

Enough big government already.

"Government is like a baby, an alimentary canal with a big appetite at one end and no sense of responsibility at the other."

-Ronald Reagan-

"A government big enough to give you everything you want is big enough to take everything you have."

-Barry Goldwater-

We are not a socialist country, we are a democratic republic. So we should stop relying and expecting the government to handle all of our personal issues. With that in mind, just how big does the government need to be? They are currently the largest employer in the United States, over 20,000,000 (twenty million) employees. How involved should they be in our daily lives? Well according to the Constitution and our founding fathers not much. That's right. The Federal government has been steadily growing, taking more and more control of our daily lives.

A recent poll showed that fifty seven percent (57%) of Americans feel the government is too involved in issues. The Federal government has a proper and much needed place, of course. For international relations, trade negotiations, common defense, interstate commerce, overall health and welfare. Key issues which deal with the greater good of all. But, not to regulate what you watch, read, think... That is why we have smaller governments to deal with local issues.

This seems to be another issue people sit around and discuss. Even politicians have jumped on the bandwagon, at least during elections. It is not too late to demand a reduction of government and its involvement in our daily lives. We just need to remind our elected officials who they serve and what their primary guideline is to follow, when running the nation, The Constitution.

10.

States rights.

"I consider the foundation of the Constitution as laid on this ground: That 'all powers not delegated to the United States, by the Constitution, nor prohibited by it to the States, are reserved to the States or to the people' (10th Amendment). To take a single step beyond the boundaries thus specifically drawn around the powers of Congress, is to take possession of a boundless field of power, no longer susceptible to any definition."

-Thomas Jefferson-

"If a radical devolution of powers was possible, it would have been done before. The assumption of states' rights is gone. There's no support for it in the Supreme Court and there's no support for it in public opinion."

-James Q. Wilson-

The way our system of government was setup is far different from what it has become. The federal government now controls almost every aspect of the daily workings of the individual states. The federal government dictates speed limits, environmental regulations, educational standards, taxation, transportation, employment standards... all of which may be good as standalone issues. But in fact should be up to the individual states to interpret and enforce.

According to the Tenth Amendment of the Constitution the individual states and the people of which have the final authority. The authority of both state and federal government is laid out in fuller detail in Article 1, Section 10. The Federal government only has the powers given to it by the Constitution. Everything else falls to the states to dictate how laws should be enacted, enforced, and interpreted.

Our founding fathers had a strong lack of trust in an overly powerful centralized government and that is why the Constitution is set with strong checks and balances. All one needs to do is read the Bill of Rights and you will clearly see this as true. The fear was just as justified almost 220 years ago when the Constitution was ratified as it is now. The removal of the states power started before the World War One and continues to be eroded today. The people need to wake up and remind the government what their original position was before we become more socialist and lose our sense of self.

11.

Taxation, revamp the tax system.

"When more of the people's sustenance is exacted through the form of taxation than is necessary to meet the just obligations of government, such exaction becomes ruthless extortion and a violation of the fundamental principles of a free government".

-<u>Grover Cleveland</u>-

"The income tax created more criminals than any other single act of government."

-<u>Barry Goldwater</u>-

The current system of taxation not only is it inefficient it may go against the Constitution as well. The original revenue collecting agency in the US was the Customs service. They collected taxes and tariffs for goods and services which passed through the borders of our nation, paid for the services the Federal government provided. Now Article 1, section 8 of the Constitution clearly defines how revenue is to be created and does give Congress the power of taxation, Amendment 16 does give congress the authority to collect income tax.

However, with the current tax codes it is impossible to even begin to understand how the system of taxation is monitored, implemented, or operates. There are entire libraries dedicated to the tax laws. We currently have taxes for everything, marriage, death, inheritance, income, property, the list goes on. A company is taxed when it purchases a product to manufacture something, the buyer is taxed when they purchase it to sell, we are taxed when we by it, and your kids are taxed when you pass it on to them... So basically the government collects taxes on the same item at least four times, if not more. This is not right and everyone seems to agree but no one pushes the government to change this.

The simple solution is a flat point of sale tax, say ten percent. Not your income, or your property every year, but at the point of purchase. In a nation of almost 300,000,000 (three hundred million) at least 200,000,000 are shopping and making purchases. Not including tourist. So as

a basic example, if you count up everything we buy clothing, food, gas, (not including big ticket items like cars and
houses) at least $5,000.00 could be collected per person.
200,000,000 times 5,000 equals $1,000,000,000,000.00.
Now if you were to include the big ticket items, the corpo-
rations, and tourist you could easily collect 20 times that
figure. Plus I failed to include duty collected from import
tariffs, government contracts to foreign governments. The
local and state government would get their fair percent-
age, plus they collect revenue from permits, fines, tickets,
and such. We could be out of 'debt' in a couple of years,
or less.

12.

Gold Standard, we need to back our currency.

"All the perplexities, confusion and distress in America arise, not from defects in their Constitution or Confederation, not from want of honor or virtue, so much as from the downright ignorance of the nature of coin, credit and circulation."

-John Adams-

"In the absence of the gold standard, there is no way to protect savings from confiscation through inflation. There is no safe store of value."

-Alan Greenspan-

The Gold standard was a monetary standard for the basic unit of currency being equal in value to and exchangeable for a specified amount of gold. Up until the 1930's our currency was backed by the Gold Standard, which we implemented around 1900. Then during the depression that was changed. In 1933, in an effort to fight deflation congress and President Roosevelt suspended the gold standard except for foreign exchange, revoked gold as universal legal tender for debts, and banned private ownership of significant amounts of gold coin. Various acts were instituted which included Executive Order 6073, the Emergency Banking Act, Executive Order 6102, Executive Order 6111, the Agricultural Adjustment Act, 1933 Banking Act, House Joint Resolution 192, and the Gold Reserve Act. Though many challenged these actions, they were upheld by the US Supreme Court in the "Gold Clause Cases" in 1935.

Somehow we have managed to accumulate some astronomical amount of debt. This stems from incompetent financial management, overspending, excessive printing of monies, and unfair trade practices. We loan billions and billions of dollars to foreign nations, we have a history of forgiving these debts, we allow foreign governments to buy our t-bills and bonds, and we continue to spend much needed money overseas. All the while our dollar falls and our economy crumbles.

We live in such a great nation with numerous resources and such, there is absolutely no excuse to be in the position we are. All we need to do is back our currencies against our resources and challenge other nations to do the same. It may not be realistic to return to the Gold Standard, there is not enough gold to back our dollar currently in circulation much less the other world economies, however, if you combine all our resources we are far wealthier than any other nation.

13.

Oil and other resources.

"It has become appallingly obvious that our technology has exceeded our humanity."

-Albert Einstein-

"We should increase our development of alternative fuels, taking advantage of renewable resources, like using corn and sugar to produce ethanol or soybeans to produce biodiesel."

-Bobby Jindal-

One of America's strengths is our abundance of resources, not just natural but 'human' innovation. A strong can do spirit. We are a nation of very capable people from many diverse backgrounds. When we as a whole set out to accomplish something, we do. Some of the most creative, out-of-the-box thinkers either are or have been American. That is what sets us apart, we see opportunity in the most unusual circumstance and that is largely due to having the freedom to try.

We have some of the richest most fertile land. When one looks at our overall food production we have it all. Fruits, vegetables, grains (wheat, barley, oats...), meats (beef, pork, chicken...), fish, seafood, you name it somewhere in the US we can produce it. We could feed the world and reap the financial benefits to help improve our quality of life.

Other resources, both renewable and nonrenewable, include but are not limited to lumber, steel, ore, precious metals, coal, fossil fuels (some of the largest shale oil reserves on the planet), energy (wind, solar, hydro, nuclear...). We could actually be self-sufficient. We would never need to rely on any foreign power if we would just properly use and recycle what we have. We in fact should be selling our resources and at the same time creating innovative means to function with alternative products, instead of relying on foreign products.

14.

America's education system.

"The aim of education is the knowledge
not of fact, but of values."

-Dean William R. Inge-

"A tax-supported, compulsory educational system
is the complete model of the totalitarian state".

-Isabel Paterson-

The current education system as it exists today is a travesty. It does not cater to the needs of the student nor to the needs of society in the various communities. The current education system is geared towards financing. The main goals of the school board and the department of education are clearly geared towards getting Federal funding for the school and its programs.

The Federal Government has laid out a system that all schools must comply with or risk a reduction in funding. These are cloaked with various titles over the years such as outcome-based education or standardized testing. Each state is required to administer state achievement tests which are standardized tests required in all public schools for the schools to receive federal funding, this is according to the Elementary and Secondary Education Act of 1965, in US Public Law 107-110, and the No Child Left Behind Act of 2001.

Though these may seem fair, they in fact are not and even put the students on unfair levels. It is a simple fact that some people are just better learners than others. It is also a fact that some parents take a deeper interest into their child's growth and development than others. It also does not reflect on the needs of the communities. Parents have been losing their rights to dictate what the course of study should be in the classroom. They are often discouraged from participating because the school board is obligated to follow a system that simply is not beneficial to the student or the community.

15.

Frivolous lawsuits and insurance claims.

"Frivolous lawsuits are booming in this county. The U.S. has more costs of litigation per person than any other industrialized nation in the world, and it is crippling our economy."

-Jack Kingston-

"Actually lowering the cost of insurance would be accomplished by such things as making it harder for lawyers to win frivolous lawsuits against insurance companies."

-Thomas Sowell-

The courts need to be held accountable for the high cost of products and services. When you subtract a fair wage for goods and services provided, the daily cost of doing business, and the inventory necessary to provide said service or product we still come up with added cost. Where does this come from? The answer is simple, and we see it all the time in the daily news.

Stop all of those frivolous lawsuits and use insurance as it was intended, for emergencies. When an elderly woman spills hot coffee and sues because, well, it was hot, we pay. When a burglar breaks his leg breaking into a house and sues the homeowner, we pay. When someone who lives in a flood plain and the home gets flooded, we pay. This goes back to personal responsibility. Everyone knows that coffee (unless you are buying iced coffee) is hot. If someone breaks into your home and gets hurt, that isn't the home owner's fault, that's karma cloaked as justice. If you live in an area that gets hurricanes, tornados, floods, locust, almost every year, move.

But the way things go we allow these and other actions to go unpunished. From the lawyers who take on these cases, the judges who try them, the insurance companies who pay, and the ones who initiated the action all need to be held accountable. Instead of our insurance premiums going up, or the cost of a product going up those who try and sue for frivolous nonsense need to be fined and punished accordingly.

16.

Revamp the justice
& prison system.

"At his best, man is the noblest of all animals;
separated from law and justice he is the worst."

"The virtue of justice consists in moderation,
as regulated by wisdom."

-Aristotle-

We currently have extremely overcrowded prisons. A statement that is far too obvious. But we currently have over 7,000,000 (seven million) people currently tied up in the corrections system. It cost the American tax payer almost $200,000,000,000.00 (two-hundred billion) a year. That comes to approximately $30,000.00 per inmate. This is more than the average yearly salary for many people, who's hard earned tax dollars, are paying the bill.

So, there are many ways to look at this. When you commit a crime that goes against the laws of the nation/society which you are a part of, you are to be punished. Everyone would seem to agree with that point. So why do many inmates actually live better than honest people? They get cable TV, full medical, clothing, beds, meals, education, a small wage, why not be a criminal? Getting caught doesn't sound so bad. Many appeal their sentences, three or four times, wasting tax dollars and taking years to process. Inmates can sit on death row for twelve to twenty years, all the while getting the benefits.

The prison system needs to be seriously overhauled. Do away with the special privileges, and excessive appeals. Many may not approve of the death penalty but, there is a reason that sentence was handed out. They had their appeal. Remember the saying 'do the crime do the time'. If they are illegal or a foreign national, send them home and bill the foreign government for all expenses. For lesser crimes there are other alternatives as well fines, community service, and military service.

17.

Illegal aliens... key word illegal.

"Emergency health care for illegal aliens along
the southwestern border is already costing
area hospitals $200 million a year, with perhaps
another $100 million in extended care costs."

-Gary Miller-

"Our nation's immigration policy has been of top
concern in recent years, and for good reason. With
between eight and twelve million illegal aliens in the
United States, it is obviously a problem out of control."

-Chris Cannon-

Perhaps almost every American can trace their roots back to a ship that traveled across the ocean to tame a 'savage land', so the story goes. But they fought, bled, and died to create the nation we now call home. Thousands came in search of a new home, earning everything they got. Just as we now get to reap the benefit of their hardships by being born here. For those who are not so lucky we have a system in place to legalize anyone wishing to become a citizen. It may take time and there are rules and regulations but, in the end they will have earned their right.

As for anyone else, if there is a deep seated desire to better your status and position good for you. But don't sneak into another country and become a burden. Illegal aliens are called illegal for a reason, they broke the law, they violated our property by crossing over into this land. Just the same way if someone snuck into your house and lived in the attic. They are trespassing, the police would be called, and the trespasser would be prosecuted. Same should be done to illegal aliens. They should not be rewarded.

They have not earned their right to our welfare programs, education benefits, hospital care, drivers licenses, unemployment benefits, or any other program that is supported/financed by honest hard working legal taxpaying citizens.   If they wish to earn their right to be in the United States, then do it the right way, apply and wait. I would also support military service. You serve in Iraq or Afghanistan you then clearly would have earned your right.

18.

The Armed Forces.

"Freedom does not come without a price. We may sometimes take for granted the many liberties we enjoy in America, but they have all been earned through the ultimate sacrifice paid by so many of the members of our armed forces."

-Charlie Dent-

"I'm inclined to think that a military background wouldn't hurt anyone."

-William Faulkner-

There is a strong misconception that the armed forces are filled with the dumb poor detriments of society. In fact many of the people who serve are educated and come from well off families. Or they are smart enough to take advantage of the benefits which are provided for their service and possible sacrifice. Now, we all know that many still may fit the image. The military provides an escape from an otherwise negative path. One needs to remember that we currently have an all voluntary force no one is forced to join.

That is one of the things that make our military so strong. It also creates recruiting issues. This is not the case in many countries around the world, military service is mandatory at 18 or after the completion of university. In a nation of 300,000,000 it can still be hard to recruit, especially in time of war. The recruiters compete with much better paying civilian jobs, anti-war personalities, and other factors. All of which limits the pool that recruiters draw from.

Well many nations have foreign legions, the most obvious is France. If we were to institute a foreign legion with the promise of citizenship we could reduce the strain on current reserves. Illegal aliens could be granted amnesty and have citizenship granted after the completion of honorable service, which would be fully earned. Then we have another place to recruit from, the overcrowded prisons. Many people are serving time for small crimes, society would benefit from their service much more than incarceration. It would still be voluntary and after the completion of honorable service, they would have earned a fresh start.

19.

Fix our infrastructure first.

"A successful society is characterized by a rising living standard for its population, increasing investment in factories and basic infrastructure, and the generation of additional surplus, which is invested in generating new discoveries in science and technology."

-Robert Trout-

"If our country is serious about reducing our dependency on foreign oil, we need to get serious about mobilizing the infrastructure necessary to distribute and dispense the next generation of fuels."

-Bart Gordon-

Though this issue has been touched on throughout previously mentioned issues, it is still something our politicians have seemed to conveniently forget. Prior to any good election they all go to the inner cities and say that there is a serious problem. They will go to some flood zone, hurricane disaster, or forest fire, whatever is the issue in the district they are trying to be elected from. They make all these ridiculous promises and say all the right words, leave you with the feeling of 'wow this one cares'.

Then they are in office... well of course it takes time to fix all the mistakes of the previous officials. Well then we can't forget funding. After a while we realize that it was all smoke with no substance. The elected officials either don't care or something really important has arisen, ok most of us can accept that. But then why is it ok to spend billions to fix up someone else's country? Water wells are drilled in drought stricken country X, what about our own droughts and the need for new wells? Hospitals and schools are refurbished in country X, what the ones in our country (that were promised to be funded)?

It is long past overdue that we hold our elected officials accountable to the needs of our society. We have overcrowded schools, dilapidated bridges, and outdated electrical facilities. America has reached a point in time where we need to spend our tax dollars in our country. Use our resources and contracts to rebuild our infrastructure. How can we set the example if we don't live up to the set standard? It is time to fix America.

20.

Stop the political correctness.

"A nation can survive its fools and even the ambitious. But it cannot survive treason from within. An enemy at the gates is less formidable, for he is known and he carries his banners openly against the city. But the traitor moves among those within the gates freely, his sly whispers rustling through all alleys, heard in the very halls of government itself. For the traitor appears no traitor; he speaks in the accents familiar to his victim, and he wears their face and their garments and he appeals to the baseness that lies deep in the hearts of all men. He rots the soul of a nation; he works secretly and unknown in the night to undermine the pillars of a city; he infects the body politic so that it can no longer resist. A murderer is less to be feared. The traitor is the plague."

-Cicero-

Perhaps it served its purpose when it first erupted on the social scene in the 1980's. We had reached a point that people were very tired of the jokes and stereotyping of cultures and various groups of people. Both Hollywood and the music industry were built on the exploitation of diverse groups. No group was safe though, it wasn't just racial, religious, cultural, it also reached the mentally handicapped, and elderly.

So then the overly conscience minded started to push for the halt to anything which pointed out the stereotyped attributes of any group. Regardless if these traits were in fact based on truth, it was deemed offensive and inappropriate to label anyone or speak about such things. A whole society was changed by this train of thought which was not just limited to the entertainment fields but extended to law enforcement as well. By the 1990s it was called profiling.

Now at what point does an entire society cross over from trying to treat everyone equally to actually dictating what is proper. Profiling was a long standing law enforcement tool used to track criminal elements. This was for the greater benefit of all society. Though it can be argued it was sometimes abused, the same can be said for the now politically correct. The first Amendment of our great Constitution guarantees freedom of expression. So it should fall on the listener as whether they wish to partake in the current discussion. Proper upbringing and teaching should be what is needed, not government enforced political correctness.

21.

The bias news media.

"To hell with the news. I'm no longer interested in news. I'm interested in causes. We don't print the truth. We don't pretend to print the truth..."

-Ben Bradlee-

"The mainstream media has its own agenda. They do not want to print the facts. They have an agenda, they have a slant, they have a bias. It is outrageous to me."

-Curt Weldon-

Freedom of speech is one thing but when a public organization is in a position of influence over a populace it should return to the days of fair reporting. We all have heard the saying that there are three sides to every story yours, mine and, the truth. Well that should be especially true for what is reported on the nightly news. But, there seems to be growing trend to move away from fair and equal reporting to a more opinionated and bias reporting style.

These arguments are nothing new, actually they were relevant in the dawn of the modern electronic media outlets, perhaps even in the time of the town crier. This need to regulate the media resulted in the creation of the Federal Communications Commission (FCC) in 1934. There have been many laws passed since which include The National Television Ownership Rule (1941), Dual Network Rule (1946), Local Television Ownership Rule (1964), Television-Radio Cross Ownership Rule (1970), and the Broadcast-Newspaper Cross Ownership Prohibition (1975) all geared at keeping fair coverage of information.

But, then in the 1980's the government started deregulating the media outlets. This continues even now but, there are so many outlets available newspapers, magazines, radio, television, cable, internet, cell phones, and don't forget advertisement billboards. So one would think that the reporting is non-biased but that is not the case. The major companies still own the larger media outlets and present the stories they see fit. I am all for freedom of speech, but when a few have the power of informational influence over the majority, that is not right.

22.

National security.

"The Constitution and Bill of Right, as increasing numbers of conservatives are beginning to see, are viewed as obstacles to be overcome by the Socialist programs our radical egalitarians wish to continue and expand. Those that truly revere the Constitution and Republic that was originally established on this continent certainly cannot continue to coexist indefinitely with those that, like their abolitionist progenitors, burned the Constitution and did everything in their power to subvert it."

-Wayne Carlson-

"For a people who are free, and who mean to remain so, a well-organized and armed militia is their best security."

-Thomas Jefferson-

This is one can be viewed as a double edged sword in a free society. We pride ourselves in being the freest nation on the planet. We live in fear of attacks from an unseen enemy, one that is very real, yet the average American has never seen. Instead we live by the newly created Department of Homeland Securities 'Homeland Security Advisory System', a list of colors telling us of the dangers.

Instead of creating some elementary school color chart they should be actively securing the borders, hunting possible terrorist, and keeping the fight to the enemy. I do commend them on doing what they can, with the limited resources at their disposal. The problem is that we as Americans don't like the intrusion into our personal freedoms. We have the right to speak as we wish, to bear arms, freedom of movement, free from governmental abuse, and we have to right to be secure in our homes. So where does the balance come in? Well since most of us are good Americans, live our lives, perhaps even served this great nation ourselves, we have nothing to fear.

But we as citizens need to allow the law enforcement agencies to do their job. Not interfere because the rights of some non-US citizen might be violated. Stop condemning the various agencies and the military for doing what needs to be done. If you are a good person, you should have nothing to fear. If you are a bad person, well then you get what you deserve. That use to be the popular thought in this country, time to return to it. Our security needs to be top priority not those who wish us harm rights.

23.

Allow the military fight.

"Still, if you will not fight for the right when you can easily win without bloodshed; if you will not fight when your victory will be sure and not too costly; you may come to the moment when you will have to fight with all the odds against you and only a precarious chance of survival. There may even be a worse case. You may have to fight when there is no hope of victory, because it is better to perish than live as slaves."

-Winston Churchill-

"Diplomats are just as essential to starting a war as soldiers are for finishing it... "

-Will Rogers-

We have the finest fighting force on the planet. Some of the best technology ever used in warfare. The finest trained and disciplined troops, with the most highly educated and trained leadership. Our intelligence agencies are the envy of the world. We have satellites that can read the headlines off newspapers, strategic missiles hitting targets a thousand miles away, so many airplanes we could block out the sun, enough nukes to blow up the planet ten times and yet we haven't won the war(s) yet?

Well the number one problem with any successful military campaign is not morale, public opinion, supply/resupply, personnel, logistics, military leadership or anything so obvious. It is the intervention of the politicians. They are the ones who deploy troops for war, peacekeeping, humanitarian aid, or for whatever reason. They dictate how the Generals will utilize their troops, dictate the rules of engagement (regardless if the enemy has rules), and condemn them for using too much force.

Is it not the objective of any armed force, when sent into combat action, to win? So why does Congress hobble our leadership? Once the order is given to attack the politicians should stay out of the way until it is over then, and only then, step in and begin the political process. We have seen the mistakes of politicians who try to dictate military matters to many times. It is because the politicians that the Cold War started, The Korean War was over, Vietnam could have been won, the intervention in the Gulf War led to its sequel. It is time to let the dogs of war fight or stop releasing them.

24.

The war on drugs.

"Once brave politicians and others explain the war on drugs' true cost, the American people will scream for a cease-fire. Bring the troops home, people will urge. Treat drugs as a health problem, not as a matter for the criminal justice system."

-Larry Elder-

"We first fought the heathens in the name of religion, then Communism, and now in the name of drugs and terrorism. Our excuses for global domination always change."

-Serj Tankian-

Ok, as anyone will tell you this has really taken a back-seat to the 'War on Terror', with good reason of course. Sure the drug cartels will fight the police agencies who are investigating them but, they are not putting roadside bombs out, wearing suicide vest, or actively oppressing and combating a belief system different from their own. They are simply capitalist in the most primitive form, they have a product and we have the market. This is just simple supply and demand, economics 101.

But still it is a multi-billion dollar burden on the tax payer. As the law enforcement agencies gain technology to investigate and hopefully convict, the drug elements gain technology to combat police operations. The health care system is burdened with the treatment of drug users, often lacking the proper insurance. The courts are overburdened with drug related cases, everything from the sale/ transportation, the use of illegal drugs, domestic abuse from drug use, crimes related to both users and opposing drug elements. The jails are overcrowded from drug related convictions. Child services are burdened with the neglected and abused (physically or psychologically) children. Then we have the environmental cost of cleaning up are labs, users homes, and vehicles.

So at what point do we say the current plan of attack is not working? Education is important but it is only part of the solution. Investigating and convicting is important but it's not the only solution. Rehabilitation (at tax payer expense) has also proven to not be the correct answer.

Inner department communication/cooperation would be a good start. Allow law enforcement agencies to attack these criminal organizations at the source. We need to remember that these organizations are in fact working outside the law we wish to have enforced. Therefore, we should stop hampering the law enforcement agencies from doing what they were hired to do. In other words, just like soldiers need to be allowed to fight the 'War on Terror', law enforcement should be allow fight the "Drug War".

25.

Silent majority stop being silent.

"Democracy is two wolves and a lamb voting on what to have for lunch. Liberty is a well-armed lamb contesting the vote."

- Benjamin Franklin-

"Too often the strong, silent man is silent only because he does not know what to say, and is reputed strong only because he has remained silent".

-Winston Churchill-

Every day on the news or the internet we see, read, and hear the point of view of some commentator. They may be liberal perhaps conservative. We sit and take half of what they say before getting distracted by daily life. Often they are bashing political figures, denouncing some policy, promoting some agenda, or merely pitching the sale of their new book. Whatever it is gets tuned out by the personal cares of the individual. We are content dealing with our music, movies, games, relationships, vacation plans, and the upcoming weekend.

Then one day a new policy is presented to become law, new taxes are announced, or some politician has acted inappropriately. Everyone in the break room, jobsite, bar, and anywhere else we gather start talking about it. The debates fly on both sides of the spectrum. Everyone has an opinion, some have an informed opinion others do not, but opinions are still shared by all. The only thing this group seems to agree on is that something needs to be done.

But then... no one does. Come Election Day no one votes. No one petitions their elected officials. No one holds the elected official accountable. Instead the next week this same group of individuals will all gather and discuss the results and either complain or rejoice. But very few will actively follow through and participate in the production of change. Instead everyone just talks amongst themselves. The reason being is that at the end of the day we still have our music, movies, games, and everything that we are content with, all at the cost of our rights and freedoms.

Section III

America always overcomes the odds...

"The government, which was designed for the people, has got into the hands of the bosses and their employers, the special interests. An invisible empire has been set up above the forms of democracy."

-Woodrow Wilson-

There must be a positive passion for the public good... established in the minds of the people, or there can be no republican government, nor any real liberty: and this public passion must be superior to all private passions.

-John Adams-

Power to the people

The United States was founded by a brave and daring group of people from various backgrounds and from all walks of life. They risked the dangers of sea travel, venturing into the unknown, with only what they could carry.

Now it is common knowledge the reasons they took such risk. Perhaps they came for the chance at a new start, to flee from oppression, to seek greater financial opportunity, adventure, to find treasure, to escape persecution, running from the law, or just to see what was beyond the horizon. They came freely... or in chains gaining freedom later.

Whatever the means and/or reason they came here, they did. Over time they carved out a new life. Either by fair trade or by brute force they developed entire communities, created livelihoods, and build homesteads. In varying degrees of personal sacrifice they fought for and earned their place, their piece of America. If not for themselves then for future generations...

From these harsh beginnings a new spirit based on freedom and independence was born. In time they broke away from the old oppressive ideals of the European courts and made their own societies, which merged into organized states.

When the time was right they rose up and broke away from the kings of old. After more than a decade they finally earned their freedom and made it known to the world that there was a new nation on the map. This new nation was powerful and strong enough to stand up to the mightiest powers in Europe.

In the next couple of decades their sovereignty was challenged. But each time their mettle was tested the United States proved it was up for the challenge. Whether defending its territory, its people, its political interest, or expansion the US proved it was up for anything that came its way.

Compared to most places on the planet, the United States has a very short history. Actually the post-Columbus America has roughly 500 years of history. With what is now considered the United States having only 400 years from Plymouth Rock to now. That is nothing compared to China, Egypt, the African continent, and even our European homeland.

Think of what we have accomplished in such a short time. The United States has been victorious in the various times of strife, whether these came from economic, political, militarily, social, feast or famine. The United States has always had the resolve necessary to come out better than when it entered.

Each time there have been naysayers and doomsayers predicting the final fall of this great nation. They sit and watch with envious eyes wait for a chance for us the crumble hoping to grab the crumbs.

Our current situation is nothing new, and the outcome is just as predictable as all the past times. We just need to band together, remember our roots, remember the hardships our founding fathers and past generations endured, and realize that if they could overcome all the hardships they endured then surely The United States will bounce back from our current situation.

We just need to have the courage to ride this out, and to have the winning spirit to come out on top yet once again. But it won't be easy. We need to have faith in our leaders, yet they need to remember what their primary purpose is. Their first priority is to the American public not the foreign powers.

To make this happen it begins with you and me. Hold the elected official accountable for their actions, return to the core of our nation, the constitution, and properly voice your concerns to your elected servants.

Much of the needed changes should begin at the local level and flow uphill to the state then to the federal. But at the same time change needs to start at the top and flow back down to the hands of the people.

America was once a great nation and in no time it can be again.

Final thoughts...

If you are truly interested in the future of this great nation, either for personal gain or for the greater good, than it is time to stop thinking, wishing, and hoping for a miracle. Miracles don't just happen, they are created by ordinary people who put forth the added effort to make a difference.

They say the hardest part of any journey is the first step. Well if you are ready and willing here are a few websites to hopefully assist in the journey. These were accurate as of the time this book was written. So check out some simple links to government sites, both state and federal.

http://www.statelocalgov.net/
The State and Local Government Internet directory

http://www.senate.gov/
United States Senate

http://www.house.gov/
United States House of Representatives

http://www.usa.gov/
United States Government information/resource

http://www.constitutionfacts.com/
The US Constitution and related information

http://www.whitehouse.gov/
The White House

http://www.truelanderdreams.com
A good resource for veterans, jobseekers, and the like...

For those who may have never read the Declaration of Independence or the Constitution... now is as good of a time as any. I have included it in the following pages. Many people don't realize that these two documents go together... can't have one with the other!

Section IV

The U.S. Constitution
And
The Declaration of Independence

"The U. S. Constitution doesn't guarantee
happiness, only the pursuit of it. You
have to catch up with it yourself."

-Benjamin Franklin-

"Firearms are second only to the Constitution in
importance; they are the peoples' liberty's teeth."

-George Washington-

The Declaration of Independence

IN CONGRESS, July 4, 1776.

The unanimous Declaration of the thirteen united States of America,

When in the Course of human events, it becomes necessary for one people to dissolve the political bands which have connected them with another, and to assume among the powers of the earth, the separate and equal station to which the Laws of Nature and of Nature's God entitle them, a decent respect to the opinions of mankind requires that they should declare the causes which impel them to the separation.

We hold these truths to be self-evident, that all men are created equal, that they are endowed by their Creator with certain unalienable Rights, that among these are Life, Liberty and the pursuit of Happiness.--That to secure these rights, Governments are instituted among Men, deriving their just powers from the consent of the governed, --That whenever any Form of Government becomes destructive of these ends, it is the Right of the People to alter or to abolish it, and to institute new Government, laying its foundation on such principles and organizing its powers in such form, as to them shall seem most likely to effect their Safety and Happiness. Prudence, indeed, will dictate that Governments long established should not be changed for light and transient causes; and accordingly all experience hath shewn, that mankind are more disposed to suffer, while evils are sufferable, than to right themselves by abolishing the forms to which they are accustomed. But when a long train of abuses and usurpations, pursuing invariably the same Object evinces a design to reduce them under absolute Despotism, it is their right, it is their duty, to throw off such Government, and to provide new Guards for their future security.--Such has been the patient sufferance of these Colonies; and such is now the necessity which constrains them to alter their former Systems of Government. The history of the present King of Great Britain is a history of repeated injuries and usurpations, all having in direct object the establishment of an absolute Tyranny over these States. To prove this, let Facts be submitted to a candid world.

He has refused his Assent to Laws, the most wholesome and necessary for the public good.
He has forbidden his Governors to pass Laws of immediate and pressing importance, unless suspended in their operation till his Assent should be obtained; and when so suspended, he has utterly neglected to attend to them.
He has refused to pass other Laws for the accommodation of large districts of people, unless those people would relinquish the right of Representation in the Legislature, a right inestimable to them and formidable to tyrants only.
He has called together legislative bodies at places unusual, uncomfortable, and distant from the depository of their public Records, for the sole purpose of fatiguing them into compliance with his measures.

He has dissolved Representative Houses repeatedly, for opposing with manly firmness his invasions on the rights of the people.

He has refused for a long time, after such dissolutions, to cause others to be elected; whereby the Legislative powers, incapable of Annihilation, have returned to the People at large for their exercise; the State remaining in the mean time exposed to all the dangers of invasion from without, and convulsions within.

He has endeavoured to prevent the population of these States; for that purpose obstructing the Laws for Naturalization of Foreigners; refusing to pass others to encourage their migrations hither, and raising the conditions of new Appropriations of Lands.

He has obstructed the Administration of Justice, by refusing his Assent to Laws for establishing Judiciary powers.

He has made Judges dependent on his Will alone, for the tenure of their offices, and the amount and payment of their salaries.

He has erected a multitude of New Offices, and sent hither swarms of Officers to harrass our people, and eat out their substance.

He has kept among us, in times of peace, Standing Armies without the Consent of our legislatures.

He has affected to render the Military independent of and superior to the Civil power.

He has combined with others to subject us to a jurisdiction foreign to our constitution, and unacknowledged by our laws; giving his Assent to their Acts of pretended Legislation:

For Quartering large bodies of armed troops among us:

For protecting them, by a mock Trial, from punishment for any Murders which they should commit on the Inhabitants of these States:

For cutting off our Trade with all parts of the world:

For imposing Taxes on us without our Consent:

For depriving us in many cases, of the benefits of Trial by Jury:

For transporting us beyond Seas to be tried for pretended offences

For abolishing the free System of English Laws in a neighbouring Province, establishing therein an Arbitrary government, and enlarging its Boundaries so as to render it at once an example and fit instrument for introducing the same absolute rule into these Colonies:

For taking away our Charters, abolishing our most valuable Laws, and altering fundamentally the Forms of our Governments:

For suspending our own Legislatures, and declaring themselves invested with power to legislate for us in all cases whatsoever.

He has abdicated Government here, by declaring us out of his Protection and waging War against us.

He has plundered our seas, ravaged our Coasts, burnt our towns, and destroyed the lives of our people.

He is at this time transporting large Armies of foreign Mercenaries to compleat the works of death, desolation and tyranny, already begun with circumstances of Cruelty & perfidy scarcely paralleled in the most barbarous ages, and totally unworthy the Head of a civilized nation.

He has constrained our fellow Citizens taken Captive on the high Seas to bear Arms against their Country, to become the executioners of their friends and Brethren, or to fall themselves by their Hands.

He has excited domestic insurrections amongst us, and has endeavoured to bring on the inhabitants of our frontiers, the merciless Indian Savages, whose known rule of warfare, is an undistinguished destruction of all ages, sexes and conditions.

In every stage of these Oppressions We have Petitioned for Redress in the most humble terms: Our repeated Petitions have been answered only by repeated injury. A Prince whose character is thus marked by every act which may define a Tyrant, is unfit to be the ruler of a free people.

Nor have We been wanting in attentions to our Brittish brethren. We have warned them from time to time of attempts by their legislature to extend an unwarrantable jurisdiction over us. We have reminded them of the circumstances of our emigration and settlement here. We have appealed to their native justice and magnanimity, and we have conjured them by the ties of our common kindred to disavow these usurpations, which, would inevitably interrupt our connections and correspondence. They too have been deaf to the voice of justice and of consanguinity. We must, therefore, acquiesce in the necessity, which denounces our Separation, and hold them, as we hold the rest of mankind, Enemies in War, in Peace Friends.

We, therefore, the Representatives of the united States of America, in General Congress, Assembled, appealing to the Supreme Judge of the world for the rectitude of our intentions, do, in the Name, and by Authority of the good People of these Colonies, solemnly publish and declare, That these United Colonies are, and of Right ought to be Free and Independent States; that they are Absolved from all Allegiance to the British Crown, and that all political connection between them and the State of Great Britain, is and ought to be totally dissolved; and that as Free and Independent States, they have full Power to levy War, conclude Peace, contract Alliances, establish Commerce, and to do all other Acts and Things which Independent States may of right do. And for the support of this Declaration, with a firm reliance on the protection of divine Providence, we mutually pledge to each other our Lives, our Fortunes and our sacred Honor.

The 56 signatures on the Declaration:

Georgia:
Button Gwinnett
Lyman Hall
George Walton
North Carolina:
William Hooper
Joseph Hewes
John Penn
South Carolina:
Edward Rutledge
Thomas Heyward, Jr.

Thomas Lynch, Jr.

Arthur Middleton

Massachusetts:

John Hancock

Maryland:

Samuel Chase

William Paca

Thomas Stone

Charles Carroll of Carrollton

Virginia:

George Wythe

Richard Henry Lee

Thomas Jefferson

Benjamin Harrison

Thomas Nelson, Jr.

Francis Lightfoot Lee

Carter Braxton

Pennsylvania:

Robert Morris

Benjamin Rush

Benjamin Franklin

John Morton

George Clymer

James Smith

George Taylor

James Wilson

George Ross

Delaware:

Caesar Rodney

George Read

Thomas McKean

New York:

William Floyd

Philip Livingston

Francis Lewis

Lewis Morris

New Jersey:

Richard Stockton

John Witherspoon

Francis Hopkinson

John Hart

Abraham Clark

New Hampshire:

Josiah Bartlett

William Whipple

Massachusetts:

Samuel Adams

John Adams

Robert Treat Paine

Elbridge Gerry

Rhode Island:

Stephen Hopkins

William Ellery

Connecticut:

Roger Sherman

Samuel Huntington

William Williams

Oliver Wolcott

New Hampshire:

Matthew Thornton

The Constitution of the United States

The signing of the Constitution took place on September 17, 1787, at the Pennsylvania State House (now called Independence Hall) in Philadelphia.

PREAMBLE

We the People of the United States, in Order to form a more perfect Union, establish Justice, insure domestic Tranquility, provide for the common defense, promote the general Welfare, and secure the Blessings of Liberty to ourselves and our Posterity, do ordain and establish this Constitution for the United States of America.

Article I.

Section 1. THE LEGISLATIVE BRANCH

All legislative Powers herein granted shall be vested in a Congress of the United States, which shall consist of a Senate and House of Representatives.

Section 2. THE HOUSE OF REPRESENTATIVES

[1] The House of Representatives shall be composed of Members chosen every second Year by the People of the several States, and the Electors in each State shall have the Qualifications requisite for Electors of the most numerous Branch of the State Legislature.

[2] No Person shall be a Representative who shall not have attained to the Age of twenty-five Years, and been seven Years a Citizen of the United States, and who shall not, when elected, be an Inhabitant of that State in which he shall be chosen.

[3] [Representatives and direct Taxes shall be apportioned among the several States which may be included within this Union, according to their respective Numbers, which shall be determined by adding to the whole Number of free Persons, including those bound to Service for a Term of Years, and excluding Indians not taxed, three fifths of all other Persons.] *(Note: Changed by section 2 of the Fourteenth Amendment.)* The actual Enumeration shall be made within three Years after the first Meeting of the Congress of the United States, and within every subsequent Term of ten Years, in such Manner as they shall by Law direct. The Number of Representatives shall not exceed one for every thirty Thousand, but each State shall have at Least one Representative; and until such enumeration shall be made, the State of New Hampshire shall be entitled to chuse three, Massachusetts eight, Rhode-Island and Providence Plantations one, Connecticut five, New-York six, New Jersey four, Pennsylvania eight, Delaware one, Maryland six, Virginia ten, North Carolina five, South Carolina five, and Georgia three.

[4] When vacancies happen in the Representation from any state, the Executive Authority thereof shall issue Writs of Election to fill such Vacancies.

[5] The House of Representatives shall chuse their Speaker and other Officers; and shall have the sole Power of Impeachment.

Section 3. THE SENATE

[1] The Senate of the United States shall be composed of two Senators from each State, [chosen by the Legislature thereof,] *(Note: Changed by section 1 of the Seventeenth Amendment.)* for six Years; and each Senator shall have one Vote.

[2] Immediately after they shall be assembled in Consequence of the first Election, they shall be divided as equally as may be into three Classes. The Seats of the Senators of the first Class shall be vacated at the Expiration of the second Year, of the second Class at the Expiration of the fourth Year, and of the third Class at the Expiration of the sixth Year, so that one-third may be chosen every second Year; [and if Vacancies happen by Resignation, or otherwise, during the Recess of the Legislature of any State, the Executive thereof may make temporary Appointments until the next Meeting of the Legislature, which shall then fill such Vacancies.] *(Note: Changed by clause 2 of the Seventeenth Amendment.)*

[3] No Person shall be a Senator who shall not have attained to the Age of thirty Years, and been nine Years a Citizen of the United States, and who shall not, when elected, be an Inhabitant of that State for which he shall be chosen.

[4] The Vice President of the United States shall be President of the Senate, but shall have no Vote, unless they be equally divided.

[5] The Senate shall chuse their other Officers, and also a President pro tempore, in the Absence of the Vice President, or when he shall exercise the Office of President of the United States.

[6] The Senate shall have the sole Power to try all Impeachments. When sitting for that Purpose, they shall be on Oath or Affirmation. When the President of the United States is tried, the Chief Justice shall preside: And no Person shall be convicted without the Concurrence of two thirds of the Members present.

[7] Judgment in Cases of Impeachment shall not extend further than to removal from Office, and disqualification to hold and enjoy any Office of honor, Trust or Profit under the United States: but the Party convicted shall nevertheless be liable and subject to Indictment, Trial, Judgment and Punishment, according to Law.

Section 4. THE ORGANIZATION OF CONGRESS

[1] The Times, Places and Manner of holding Elections for Senators and Representatives, shall be prescribed in each State by the Legislature thereof; but the Congress may at any time by Law make or alter such Regulations, except as to the Place of Chusing Senators.

[2] The Congress shall assemble at least once in every Year, and such Meeting shall be [on the first Monday in December,] *(Note: Changed by section 2 of the Twentieth Amendment.)* unless they shall by Law appoint a different Day.

Section 5.

[1] Each House shall be the Judge of the Elections, Returns and Qualifications of its own Members, and a Majority of each shall constitute a Quorum to do Business; but a smaller number may adjourn from day to day, and may be authorized to compel the Attendance of absent Members, in such Manner, and under such Penalties as each House may provide.

[2] Each House may determine the Rules of its Proceedings, punish its Members for disorderly Behavior, and, with the Concurrence of two thirds, expel a Member.

[3] Each House shall keep a Journal of its Proceedings, and from time to time publish the same, excepting such Parts as may in their Judgment require Secrecy; and the Yeas and Nays of the Members of either House on any question shall, at the Desire of one fifth of those Present, be entered on the Journal.

[4] Neither House, during the Session of Congress, shall, without the Consent of the other, adjourn for more than three days, nor to any other Place than that in which the two Houses shall be sitting.

Section 6.

[1] The Senators and Representatives shall receive a Compensation for their Services, to be ascertained by Law, and paid out of the Treasury of the United States. They shall in all Cases, except Treason, Felony and Breach of the Peace, be privileged from Arrest during their Attendance at the Session of their respective Houses, and in going to and returning from the same; and for any Speech or Debate in either House, they shall not be questioned in any other Place.

[2] No Senator or Representative shall, during the Time for which he was elected, be appointed to any civil Office under the Authority of the United States, which shall have been created, or the Emoluments whereof shall have been encreased during such time; and no Person holding any Office under the United States, shall be a Member of either House during his Continuance in Office.

Section 7.

[1] All Bills for raising Revenue shall originate in the House of Representatives; but the Senate may propose or concur with Amendments as on other Bills.

[2] Every Bill which shall have passed the House of Representatives and the Senate, shall, before it become a Law, be presented to the President of the United States; If he approve he shall sign it, but if not he shall return it, with his Objections to that House in which it shall have originated,

who shall enter the Objections at large on their Journal, and proceed to reconsider it. If after such Reconsideration two thirds of that House shall agree to pass the Bill, it shall be sent, together with the Objections, to the other House, by which it shall likewise be reconsidered, and if approved by two thirds of that House, it shall become a Law. But in all such Cases the Votes of both Houses shall be determined by Yeas and Nays, and the Names of the Persons voting for and against the Bill shall be entered on the Journal of each House respectively. If any Bill shall not be returned by the President within ten Days (Sundays excepted) after it shall have been presented to him, the Same shall be a Law, in like Manner as if he had signed it, unless the Congress by their Adjournment prevent its Return, in which Case it shall not be a Law.

[3] Every Order, Resolution, or Vote to which the Concurrence of the Senate and House of Representatives may be necessary (except on a question of Adjournment) shall be presented to the President of the United States; and before the Same shall take Effect, shall be approved by him, or being disapproved by him, shall be repassed by two thirds of the Senate and House of Representatives, according to the Rules and Limitations prescribed in the Case of a Bill.

Section 8. POWERS GRANTED TO CONGRESS

[1] The Congress shall have Power To lay and collect Taxes, Duties, Imposts and Excises, to pay the Debts and provide for the common Defence and general Welfare of the

United States; but all Duties, Imposts and Excises shall be uniform throughout the United States;

[2] To borrow money on the credit of the United States;

[3] To regulate Commerce with foreign Nations, and among the several States, and with the Indian Tribes;

[4] To establish an uniform Rule of Naturalization, and uniform Laws on the subject of Bankruptcies throughout the United States;

[5] To coin Money, regulate the Value thereof, and of foreign Coin, and fix the Standard of Weights and Measures;

[6] To provide for the Punishment of counterfeiting the Securities and current Coin of the United States;

[7] To establish Post Offices and post Roads;

[8] To promote the Progress of Science and useful Arts, by securing for limited Times to Authors and Inventors the exclusive Right to their respective Writings and Discoveries;

[9] To constitute Tribunals inferior to the supreme Court;

[10] To define and punish Piracies and Felonies committed on the high Seas, and Offenses against the Law of Nations;

[11] To declare War, grant Letters of Marque and Reprisal, and make Rules concerning Captures on Land and Water;

[12] To raise and support Armies, but no Appropriation of Money to that Use shall be for a longer Term than two Years;

[13] To provide and maintain a Navy;

[14] To make Rules for the Government and Regulation of the land and naval Forces;

[15] To provide for calling forth the Militia to execute the Laws of the Union, suppress Insurrections and repel Invasions;

[16] To provide for organizing, arming, and disciplining the Militia, and for governing such Part of them as may be employed in the Service of the United States, reserving to the States respectively, the Appointment of the Officers, and the Authority of training the Militia according to the discipline prescribed by Congress;

[17] To exercise exclusive Legislation in all Cases whatsoever, over such District (not exceeding ten Miles square) as may, by Cession of particular States, and the acceptance of Congress, become the Seat of the Government of the United States, and to exercise like Authority over all Places purchased by the Consent of the Legislature of the State in which the Same shall be, for the Erection of

Forts, Magazines, Arsenals, dock-Yards, and other needful Buildings; —And

[18] To make all Laws which shall be necessary and proper for carrying into Execution the foregoing Powers, and all other Powers vested by this Constitution in the Government of the United States, or in any Department or Officer thereof.

Section 9. POWER FORBIDDEN TO CONGRESS

[1] The Migration or Importation of such Persons as any of the States now existing shall think proper to admit, shall not be prohibited by the Congress prior to the Year one thousand eight hundred and eight, but a tax or duty may be imposed on such Importation, not exceeding ten dollars for each Person.

[2] The privilege of the Writ of Habeas Corpus shall not be suspended, unless when in Cases of Rebellion or Invasion the public Safety may require it.

[3] No Bill of Attainder or ex post facto Law shall be passed.

[4] No Capitation, or other direct, Tax shall be laid, unless in Proportion to the Census or Enumeration herein before directed to be taken. *(Note: See the Sixteenth Amendment.)*

[5] No Tax or Duty shall be laid on Articles exported from any State.

[6] No Preference shall be given by any Regulation of Commerce or Revenue to the Ports of one State over those of another: nor shall Vessels bound to, or from, one State, be obliged to enter, clear, or pay Duties in another.

[7] No Money shall be drawn from the Treasury, but in Consequence of Appropriations made by Law; and a regular Statement and Account of the Receipts and Expenditures of all public Money shall be published from time to time.

[8] No Title of Nobility shall be granted by the United States: And no Person holding any Office of Profit or Trust under them, shall, without the Consent of the Congress, accept of any present, Emolument, Office, or Title, of any kind whatever, from any King, Prince, or foreign State.

Section 10.

[1] No State shall enter into any Treaty, Alliance, or Confederation; grant Letters of Marque and Reprisal; coin Money; emit Bills of Credit; make any Thing but gold and silver Coin a Tender in Payment of Debts; pass any Bill of Attainder, ex post facto Law, or Law impairing the Obligation of Contracts, or grant any Title of Nobility.

[2] No State shall, without the Consent of the Congress, lay any Imposts or Duties on Imports or Exports, except what may be absolutely necessary for executing its inspection Laws: and the net Produce of all Duties and Imposts, laid by any State on Imports or Exports, shall be for the Use of

the Treasury of the United States; and all such Laws shall be subject to the Revision and Controul of the Congress.

[3] No State shall, without the Consent of Congress, lay any duty of Tonnage, keep Troops, or Ships of War in time of Peace, enter into any Agreement or Compact with another State, or with a foreign Power, or engage in War, unless actually invaded, or in such imminent Danger as will not admit of delay.

Article II.

THE EXECUTIVE BRANCH

Section 1.

[1] The executive Power shall be vested in a President of the United States of America. He shall hold his Office during the Term of four Years, and, together with the Vice-President, chosen for the same Term, be elected, as follows.

[2] Each State shall appoint, in such Manner as the Legislature thereof may direct, a Number of Electors, equal to the whole Number of Senators and Representatives to which the State may be entitled in the Congress: but no Senator or Representative, or Person holding an Office of Trust or Profit under the United States, shall be appointed an Elector.

[3] [The Electors shall meet in their respective States, and vote by Ballot for two persons, of whom one at least shall

not be an Inhabitant of the same State with themselves. And they shall make a List of all the Persons voted for, and of the Number of Votes for each; which List they shall sign and certify, and transmit sealed to the Seat of the Government of the United States, directed to the President of the Senate. The President of the Senate shall, in the Presence of the Senate and House of Representatives, open all the Certificates, and the Votes shall then be counted. The Person having the greatest Number of Votes shall be the President, if such Number be a Majority of the whole Number of Electors appointed; and if there be more than one who have such Majority, and have an equal Number of Votes, then the House of Representatives shall immediately chuse by Ballot one of them for President; and if no Person have a Majority, then from the five highest on the List the said House shall in like Manner chuse the President. But in chusing the President, the Votes shall be taken by States, the Representation from each State have one Vote; a quorum for this Purpose shall consist of a Member or Members from two thirds of the States, and a Majority of all the States shall be necessary to a Choice. In every Case, after the Choice of the President, the Person having the greatest Number of Votes of the Electors shall be the Vice President. But if there should remain two or more who have equal Votes, the Senate shall chuse from them by Ballot the Vice-President.] *(Note: Superseded by the Twelfth Amendment.)*

[4] The Congress may determine the Time of chusing the Electors, and the Day on which they shall give their

Votes; which Day shall be the same throughout the United States.

[5] No person except a natural born Citizen, or a Citizen of the United States, at the time of the Adoption of this Constitution, shall be eligible to the Office of President; neither shall any person be eligible to that Office who shall not have attained to the Age of thirty-five Years, and been fourteen Years a Resident within the United States.

[6] [In Case of the Removal of the President from Office, or of his Death, Resignation, or Inability to discharge the Powers and Duties of the said Office, the same shall devolve on the Vice President, and the Congress may by Law, provide for the Case of Removal, Death, Resignation or Inability, both of the President and Vice President, declaring what Officer shall then act as President, and such Officer shall act accordingly, until the Disability be removed, or a President shall be elected.] *(Note: Changed by the Twenty-Fifth Amendment.)*

[7] The President shall, at stated Times, receive for his Services, a Compensation, which shall neither be encreased nor diminished during the Period for which he shall have been elected, and he shall not receive within that Period any other Emolument from the United States, or any of them.

[8] Before he enter on the Execution of his Office, he shall take the following Oath or Affirmation: —"I do solemnly swear (or affirm) that I will faithfully execute the Office of

President of the United States, and will to the best of my Ability, preserve, protect and defend the Constitution of the United States."

Section 2.

[1] The President shall be Commander in Chief of the Army and Navy of the United States, and
of the Militia of the several States, when called into the actual Service of the United States; he may require the Opinion in writing, of the principal Officer in each of the executive Departments, upon any subject relating to the Duties of their respective Offices, and he shall have Power to Grant Reprieves and Pardons for Offenses against the United States, except in Cases of Impeachment.

[2] He shall have Power, by and with the Advice and Consent of the Senate, to make Treaties, provided two-thirds of the Senators present concur; and he shall nominate, and by and with the Advice and Consent of the Senate, shall appoint Ambassadors, other public Ministers and Consuls, Judges of the supreme Court, and all other Officers of the United States, whose Appointments are not herein otherwise provided for, and which shall be established by Law: but the Congress may by Law vest the Appointment of such inferior Officers, as they think proper, in the President alone, in the Courts of Law, or in the Heads of Departments.

[3] The President shall have Power to fill up all Vacancies that may happen during the Recess of the Senate,

by granting Commissions which shall expire at the End of their next Session.

Section 3.He shall from time to time give to the Congress Information of the State of the Union, and recommend to their Consideration such Measures as he shall judge necessary and expedient; he may, on extraordinary Occasions, convene both Houses, or either of them, and in Case of Disagreement between them, with Respect to the Time of Adjournment, he may adjourn them to such Time as he shall think proper; he shall receive Ambassadors and other public Ministers; he shall take Care that the Laws be faithfully executed, and shall Commission all the Officers of the United States.

Section 4.

The President, Vice President and all civil Officers of the United States, shall be removed from Office on Impeachment for, and Conviction of, Treason, Bribery, or other high Crimes and Misdemeanors.

Article III.

Section 1. THE JUDICIAL BRANCH

The judicial Power of the United States, shall be vested in one supreme Court, and in such inferior Courts as the Congress may from time to time ordain and establish. The Judges, both of the supreme and inferior Courts, shall hold their Offices during good Behaviour, and shall, at stated Times, receive for their Services, a Compensation, which shall not be diminished during their Continuance in Office.

Section 2.

[1] The judicial Power shall extend to all Cases, in Law and Equity, arising under this Constitution, the Laws of the United States, and Treaties made, or which shall be made, under their Authority; —to all Cases affecting Ambassadors, other public Ministers and Consuls; —to all Cases of admiralty and maritime Jurisdiction; —to Controversies to which the United States shall be a Party; —to Controversies between two or more States, —[between a State and Citizens of another State;—] *(Note: Changed by the Eleventh Amendment.)* between Citizens of different States; —between Citizens of the same State claiming Lands under Grants of different States, [and between a State, or the Citizens thereof, and foreign States, Citizens or Subjects.] *(Note: Changed by the Eleventh Amendment.)*

[2] In all Cases affecting Ambassadors, other public Ministers and Consuls, and those in which a State shall be Party, the supreme Court shall have original Jurisdiction. In all the other Cases before mentioned, the supreme Court shall have appellate Jurisdiction, both as to Law and Fact, with such Exceptions, and under such Regulations as the Congress shall make.

[3] The Trial of all Crimes, except in Cases of Impeachment, shall be by Jury; and such Trial shall be held in the State where the said Crimes shall have been committed;

but when not committed within any State, the Trial shall be at such Place or Places as the Congress may by Law have directed.

Section 3.

[1] Treason against the United States, shall consist only in levying War against them, or in adhering to their Enemies, giving them Aid and Comfort. No Person shall be convicted of Treason unless on the Testimony of two Witnesses to the same overt Act, or on Confession in open Court.

[2] The Congress shall have Power to declare the Punishment of Treason, but no Attainder of Treason shall work Corruption of Blood, or Forfeiture except during the Life of the Person attainted.

Article IV.

Section 1. RELATION OF THE STATES TO EACH OTHER

Full Faith and Credit shall be given in each State to the public Acts, Records, and judicial Proceedings of every other State; And the Congress may by general Laws prescribe the Manner in which such Acts, Records and Proceedings shall be proved, and the Effect thereof.

Section 2.

[1] The Citizens of each State shall be entitled to all Privileges and Immunities of Citizens in the several States.

Peter D. Fleming

[2] A Person charged in any State with Treason, Felony, or other Crime, who shall flee from Justice, and be found in another State, shall on demand of the executive Authority of the State from which he fled, be delivered up, to be removed to the State having Jurisdiction of the Crime.

[3] [No Person held to Service or Labour in one State, under the Laws thereof, escaping into another, shall, in Consequence of any Law or Regulation therein, be discharged from such Service or Labour, but shall be delivered up on Claim of the Party to whom such Service or Labour may be due.] *(Note: Superseded by the Thirteenth Amendment.)*

Section 3.

[1] New States may be admitted by the Congress into this Union; but no new State shall be formed or erected within the Jurisdiction of any other State; nor any State be formed by the Junction of two or more States, or parts of States, without the Consent of the Legislatures of the States concerned as well as of the Congress.

[2] The Congress shall have Power to dispose of and make all needful Rules and Regulations respecting the Territory or other Property belonging to the United States; and nothing in this Constitution shall be so construed as to Prejudice any Claims of the United States, or of any particular State.

Section 4.

The United States shall guarantee to every State in this Union a Republican Form of Government, and shall pro-

100

tect each of them against Invasion; and on Application of the Legislature, or of the Executive (when the Legislature cannot be convened) against domestic Violence.

Article V.

AMENDING THE CONSTITUTION

The Congress, whenever two thirds of both Houses shall deem it necessary, shall propose Amendments to this Constitution, or, on the Application of the Legislatures of two thirds of the several States, shall call a Convention for proposing Amendments, which, in either Case, shall be valid to all Intents and Purposes, as Part of this Constitution, when ratified by the Legislatures of three fourths of the several States, or by Conventions in three fourths thereof, as the one or the other Mode of Ratification may be proposed by the Congress; Provided that no Amendment which may be made prior to the Year One thousand eight hundred and eight shall in any Manner affect the first and fourth Clauses in the Ninth Section of the first Article; and that no State, without its Consent, shall be deprived of it's equal Suffrage in the Senate.

Article VI.

NATIONAL DEBTS

[1] All Debts contracted and Engagements entered into, before the Adoption of this Constitution, shall be as valid

against the United States under this Constitution, as under the Confederation.

SUPREMACY OF THE NATIONAL GOVERNMENT

[2] This Constitution, and the Laws of the United States which shall be made in Pursuance thereof; and all Treaties made, or which shall be made, under the Authority of the United States, shall be the supreme Law of the Land; and the Judges in every State shall be bound thereby, any Thing in the Constitution or Laws of any State to the Contrary notwithstanding.

[3] The Senators and Representatives before mentioned, and the Members of the several State Legislatures, and all executive and judicial Officers, both of the United States and of the several States, shall be bound by Oath or Affirmation, to support this Constitution; but no religious Test shall ever be required as a Qualification to any Office or public Trust under the United States.

Article VII.

RATIFYING THE CONSTITUTION

The Ratification of the Conventions of nine States shall be sufficient for the Establishment of this Constitution between the States so ratifying the Same.

Done in Convention by the Unanimous Consent of the States present the Seventeenth Day of September in the Year of our Lord one thousand seven hundred and Eighty seven and of the Independence of the United States of America the Twelfth.

In Witness whereof We have hereunto subscribed our Names.

George Washington-President and deputy from Virginia Attest William Jackson Secretary

New Hampshire
John Langdon
Nicholas Gilman
Massachusetts
Nathaniel Gorham
Rufus King
Connecticut
Wm. Saml. Johnson
Roger Sherman
New York
Alexander Hamilton
New Jersey
Wil: Livingston
David Brearley
Wm. Paterson
Jona: Dayton
Pennsylvania
B Franklin
Thomas Mifflin
Robt Morris
Geo. Clymer
Thos. FitzSimons
Jared Ingersoll
James Wilson
Gouv Morris Delaware
Geo: Read
Gunning Bedford jun
John Dickinson
Richard Basset
Jaco: Broom

Maryland
James McHenry
Dan of St Thos. Jenifer
Danl Carroll
Virginia
John Blair-
James Madison Jr.
North Carolina
Wm. Blount
Richd. Dobbs Spaight
Hu Williamson
South Carolina
J. Rutledge
Charles Cotesworth
Pinckney
Charles Pinckney
Pierce Butler
Georgia
William Few
Abr Baldwin

The Bill of Rights

The first ten Amendments (Bill of Rights) were ratified effective December 15, 1791.

Amendment I: Freedom of religion, speech, and the press; rights of assembly and petition:
Congress shall make no law respecting an establishment of religion, or prohibiting the free exercise thereof; or abridging the freedom of speech, or of the press, or the right of the people peaceably to assemble, and to petition the Government for a redress of grievances.

Amendment II: Right to bear arms:
A well regulated Militia, being necessary to the security of a free State, the right of the people to keep and bear Arms, *shall not be infringed*.

Amendment III: Housing of soldiers:
No Soldier shall, in time of peace be quartered in any house, without the consent of the Owner, nor in time of war, but in a manner to be prescribed by law.

Amendment IV: Search and arrest warrants:
The right of the people to be secure in their persons, houses, papers, and effects, against unreasonable searches and seizures, shall not be violated, and no Warrants shall issue, but upon probable cause, supported by Oath

or affirmation, and particularly describing the place to be searched, and the persons or things to be seized.

Amendment V: Rights in criminal cases:
No person shall be held to answer for a capital, or otherwise infamous crime, unless on a presentment or indictment of a Grand Jury, except in cases arising in the land or naval forces, or in the Militia, when in actual service in time of War or public danger; nor shall any person be subject for the same offence to be twice put in jeopardy of life or limb, nor shall be compelled in any criminal case to be a witness against himself, nor be deprived of life, liberty, or property, without due process of law; nor shall private property be taken for public use without just compensation.

Amendment VI: Rights to a fair trial:
In all criminal prosecutions, the accused shall enjoy the right to a speedy and public trial, by an impartial jury of the State and district wherein the crime shall have been committed; which district shall have been previously ascertained by law, and to be informed of the nature and cause of the accusation; to be confronted with the witnesses against him; to have compulsory process for obtaining witnesses in his favor, and to have the assistance of counsel for his defence.

Amendment VII: Rights in civil cases:
In Suits at common law, where the value in controversy shall exceed twenty dollars, the right of trial by jury shall be preserved, and no fact tried by a jury shall be other-

wise re-examined in any Court of the United States, than according to the rules of the common law.

Amendment VIII: Bails, fines, and punishments:
Excessive bail shall not be required, nor excessive fines imposed, nor cruel and unusual punishments inflicted.

Amendment IX: Rights retained by the people:
The enumeration in the Constitution of certain rights shall not be construed to deny or disparage others retained by the people.

Amendment X: Powers retained by the states and the people:
The powers not delegated to the United States by the Constitution, nor prohibited by it to the States, are reserved to the States respectively, or to the people.

The rest of the Amendments 11-27

AMENDMENT XI
Passed by Congress March 4, 1794. Ratified February 7, 1795.
Note: Article III, section 2, of the Constitution was modified by amendment 11.
The Judicial power of the United States shall not be construed to extend to any suit in law or equity, commenced or prosecuted against one of the United States by Citizens of another State, or by Citizens or Subjects of any Foreign State.

AMENDMENT XII

Passed by Congress December 9, 1803. Ratified June 15, 1804.

Note: A portion of Article II, section 1 of the Constitution was superseded by the 12th amendment.

The Electors shall meet in their respective states and vote by ballot for President and Vice-President, one of whom, at least, shall not be an inhabitant of the same state with themselves; they shall name in their ballots the person voted for as President, and in distinct ballots the person voted for as Vice-President, and they shall make distinct lists of all persons voted for as President, and of all persons voted for as Vice-President, and of the number of votes for each, which lists they shall sign and certify, and transmit sealed to the seat of the government of the United States, directed to the President of the Senate; -- the President of the Senate shall, in the presence of the Senate and House of Representatives, open all the certificates and the votes shall then be counted; -- The person having the greatest number of votes for President, shall be the President, if such number be a majority of the whole number of Electors appointed; and if no person have such majority, then from the persons having the highest numbers not exceeding three on the list of those voted for as President, the House of Representatives shall choose immediately, by ballot, the President. But in choosing the President, the votes shall be taken by states, the representation from each state having one vote; a quorum for this purpose shall consist of a member or members from two-thirds of the states, and a majority of all the states shall be necessary to a choice. [And if the House of

Representatives shall not choose a President whenever the right of choice shall devolve upon them, before the fourth day of March next following, then the Vice-President shall act as President, as in case of the death or other constitutional disability of the President. --]* The person having the greatest number of votes as Vice-President, shall be the Vice-President, if such number be a majority of the whole number of Electors appointed, and if no person have a majority, then from the two highest numbers on the list, the Senate shall choose the Vice-President; a quorum for the purpose shall consist of two-thirds of the whole number of Senators, and a majority of the whole number shall be necessary to a choice. But no person constitutionally ineligible to the office of President shall be eligible to that of Vice-President of the United States.

Superseded by section 3 of the 20th amendment.

AMENDMENT XIII
Passed by Congress January 31, 1865. Ratified December 6, 1865.
Note: A portion of Article IV, section 2, of the Constitution was superseded by the 13th amendment.

Section 1.
Neither slavery nor involuntary servitude, except as a punishment for crime whereof the party shall have been duly convicted, shall exist within the United States, or any place subject to their jurisdiction.

Section 2.
Congress shall have power to enforce this article by appropriate legislation.

AMENDMENT XIV
Passed by Congress June 13, 1866. Ratified July 9, 1868.
Note: Article I, section 2, of the Constitution was modified
by section 2 of the 14th amendment.

Section 1.
All persons born or naturalized in the United States, and
subject to the jurisdiction thereof, are citizens of the United States and of the State wherein they reside. No State
shall make or enforce any law which shall abridge the privileges or immunities of citizens of the United States; nor
shall any State deprive any person of life, liberty, or property, without due process of law; nor deny to any person
within its jurisdiction the equal protection of the laws.

Section 2.
Representatives shall be apportioned among the several
States according to their respective numbers, counting
the whole number of persons in each State, excluding Indians not taxed. But when the right to vote at any election
for the choice of electors for President and Vice-President
of the United States, Representatives in Congress, the Executive and Judicial officers of a State, or the members
of the Legislature thereof, is denied to any of the male
inhabitants of such State, being twenty-one years of age,*
and citizens of the United States, or in any way abridged,
except for participation in rebellion, or other crime, the
basis of representation therein shall be reduced in the
proportion which the number of such male citizens shall

bear to the whole number of male citizens twenty-one years of age in such State.

Section 3.

No person shall be a Senator or Representative in Congress, or elector of President and Vice-President, or hold any office, civil or military, under the United States, or under any State, who, having previously taken an oath, as a member of Congress, or as an officer of the United States, or as a member of any State legislature, or as an executive or judicial officer of any State, to support the Constitution of the United States, shall have engaged in insurrection or rebellion against the same, or given aid or comfort to the enemies thereof. But Congress may by a vote of two-thirds of each House, remove such disability.

Section 4.

The validity of the public debt of the United States, authorized by law, including debts incurred for payment of pensions and bounties for services in suppressing insurrection or rebellion, shall not be questioned. But neither the United States nor any State shall assume or pay any debt or obligation incurred in aid of insurrection or rebellion against the United States, or any claim for the loss or emancipation of any slave; but all such debts, obligations and claims shall be held illegal and void.

Section 5.

The Congress shall have the power to enforce, by appropriate legislation, the provisions of this article.
Changed by section 1 of the 26th amendment.

AMENDMENT XV
Passed by Congress February 26, 1869. Ratified February 3, 1870.

Section 1.
The right of citizens of the United States to vote shall not be denied or abridged by the United States or by any State on account of race, color, or previous condition of servitude--

Section 2.
The Congress shall have the power to enforce this article by appropriate legislation.

AMENDMENT XVI
Passed by Congress July 2, 1909. Ratified February 3, 1913.
Note: Article I, section 9, of the Constitution was modified by amendment 16.
The Congress shall have power to lay and collect taxes on incomes, from whatever source derived, without appor-tionment among the several States, and without regard to any census or enumeration.

AMENDMENT XVII
Passed by Congress May 13, 1912. Ratified April 8, 1913.
Note: Article I, section 3, of the Constitution was modified by the 17th amendment.
The Senate of the United States shall be composed of two Senators from each State, elected by the people thereof, for six years; and each Senator shall have one vote. The electors

in each State shall have the qualifications requisite for electors of the most numerous branch of the State legislatures. When vacancies happen in the representation of any State in the Senate, the executive authority of such State shall issue writs of election to fill such vacancies: *Provided*, That the legislature of any State may empower the executive thereof to make temporary appointments until the people fill the vacancies by election as the legislature may direct. This amendment shall not be so construed as to affect the election or term of any Senator chosen before it becomes valid as part of the Constitution.

AMENDMENT XVIII
Passed by Congress December 18, 1917. Ratified January 16, 1919. Repealed by amendment 21.

Section 1.
After one year from the ratification of this article the manufacture, sale, or transportation of intoxicating liquors within, the importation thereof into, or the exportation thereof from the United States and all territory subject to the jurisdiction thereof for beverage purposes is hereby prohibited.

Section 2.
The Congress and the several States shall have concurrent power to enforce this article by appropriate legislation.

Section 3.
This article shall be inoperative unless it shall have been ratified as an amendment to the Constitution by the legislatures of the several States, as provided in the Constitu-

tion, within seven years from the date of the submission hereof to the States by the Congress.

AMENDMENT XIX
Passed by Congress June 4, 1919. Ratified August 18, 1920.
The right of citizens of the United States to vote shall not be denied or abridged by the United States or by any State on account of sex.
Congress shall have power to enforce this article by appropriate legislation.

AMENDMENT XX
Passed by Congress March 2, 1932. Ratified January 23, 1933.
Note: Article I, section 4, of the Constitution was modified by section 2 of this amendment. In addition, a portion of the 12th amendment was superseded by section 3.

Section 1.
The terms of the President and the Vice President shall end at noon on the 20th day of January, and the terms of Senators and Representatives at noon on the 3d day of January, of the years in which such terms would have ended if this article had not been ratified; and the terms of their successors shall then begin.

Section 2.
The Congress shall assemble at least once in every year, and such meeting shall begin at noon on the 3d day of January, unless they shall by law appoint a different day.

Section 3.

If, at the time fixed for the beginning of the term of the President, the President elect shall have died, the Vice President elect shall become President. If a President shall not have been chosen before the time fixed for the beginning of his term, or if the President elect shall have failed to qualify, then the Vice President elect shall act as President until a President shall have qualified; and the Congress may by law provide for the case wherein neither a President elect nor a Vice President shall have qualified, declaring who shall then act as President, or the manner in which one who is to act shall be selected, and such person shall act accordingly until a President or Vice President shall have qualified.

Section 4.

The Congress may by law provide for the case of the death of any of the persons from whom the House of Representatives may choose a President whenever the right of choice shall have devolved upon them, and for the case of the death of any of the persons from whom the Senate may choose a Vice President whenever the right of choice shall have devolved upon them.

Section 5.

Sections 1 and 2 shall take effect on the 15th day of October following the ratification of this article.

Section 6.

This article shall be inoperative unless it shall have been ratified as an amendment to the Constitution by the legislatures of three-fourths of the several States within seven years from the date of its submission.

AMENDMENT XXI
Passed by Congress February 20, 1933. Ratified December 5, 1933.

Section 1.
The eighteenth article of amendment to the Constitution of the United States is hereby repealed.

Section 2.
The transportation or importation into any State, Territory, or Possession of the United States for delivery or use therein of intoxicating liquors, in violation of the laws thereof, is hereby prohibited.

Section 3.
This article shall be inoperative unless it shall have been ratified as an amendment to the Constitution by conventions in the several States, as provided in the Constitution, within seven years from the date of the submission hereof to the States by the Congress.

AMENDMENT XXII
Passed by Congress March 21, 1947. Ratified February 27, 1951.

Section 1.
No person shall be elected to the office of the President more than twice, and no person who has held the office

of President, or acted as President, for more than two years of a term to which some other person was elected President shall be elected to the office of President more than once. But this Article shall not apply to any person holding the office of President when this Article was proposed by Congress, and shall not prevent any person who may be holding the office of President, or acting as President, during the term within which this Article becomes operative from holding the office of President or acting as President during the remainder of such term.

Section 2.
This article shall be inoperative unless it shall have been ratified as an amendment to the Constitution by the legislatures of three-fourths of the several States within seven years from the date of its submission to the States by the Congress.

AMENDMENT XXIII
Passed by Congress June 16, 1960. Ratified March 29, 1961.

Section 1.
The District constituting the seat of Government of the United States shall appoint in such manner as Congress may direct:
A number of electors of President and Vice President equal to the whole number of Senators and Representatives in Congress to which the District would be entitled if it were a State, but in no event more than the least populous State; they shall be in addition to those appointed by

the States, but they shall be considered, for the purposes of the election of President and Vice President, to be electors appointed by a State; and they shall meet in the District and perform such duties as provided by the twelfth article of amendment.

Section 2.
The Congress shall have power to enforce this article by appropriate legislation.

AMENDMENT XXIV
Passed by Congress August 27, 1962. Ratified January 23, 1964.
Section 1.

The right of citizens of the United States to vote in any primary or other election for President or Vice President, for electors for President or Vice President, or for Senator or Representative in Congress, shall not be denied or abridged by the United States or any State by reason of failure to pay poll tax or other tax.

Section 2.
The Congress shall have power to enforce this article by appropriate legislation.

AMENDMENT XXV
Passed by Congress July 6, 1965. Ratified February 10, 1967.
Note: Article II, section 1, of the Constitution was affected by the 25th amendment.

Section 1.
In case of the removal of the President from office or of his death or resignation, the Vice President shall become President.

Section 2.
Whenever there is a vacancy in the office of the Vice President, the President shall nominate a Vice President who shall take office upon confirmation by a majority vote of both Houses of Congress.

Section 3.
Whenever the President transmits to the President pro tempore of the Senate and the Speaker of the House of Representatives his written declaration that he is unable to discharge the powers and duties of his office, and until he transmits to them a written declaration to the contrary, such powers and duties shall be discharged by the Vice President as Acting President.

Section 4.
Whenever the Vice President and a majority of either the principal officers of the executive departments or of such other body as Congress may by law provide, transmit to the President pro tempore of the Senate and the Speaker of the House of Representatives their written declaration that the President is unable to discharge the powers and duties of his office, the Vice President shall immediately assume the powers and duties of the office as Acting President.

Thereafter, when the President transmits to the President pro tempore of the Senate and the Speaker of the House of Representatives his written declaration that no inability exists, he shall resume the powers and duties of his office unless the Vice President and a majority of either the principal officers of the executive department or of such other body as Congress may by law provide, transmit within four days to the President pro tempore of the Senate and the Speaker of the House of Representatives their written declaration that the President is unable to discharge the powers and duties of his office. Thereupon Congress shall decide the issue, assembling within forty-eight hours for that purpose if not in session. If the Congress, within twenty-one days after receipt of the latter written declaration, or, if Congress is not in session, within twenty-one days after Congress is required to assemble, determines by two-thirds vote of both Houses that the President is unable to discharge the powers and duties of his office, the Vice President shall continue to discharge the same as Acting President; otherwise, the President shall resume the powers and duties of his office.

AMENDMENT XXVI
Passed by Congress March 23, 1971. Ratified July 1, 1971.
Note: Amendment 14, section 2, of the Constitution was modified by section 1 of the 26th amendment.

Section 1.
The right of citizens of the United States, who are eighteen years of age or older, to vote shall not be denied or

abridged by the United States or by any State on account of age.

Section 2.
The Congress shall have power to enforce this article by appropriate legislation.

AMENDMENT XXVII
Originally proposed Sept. 25, 1789. *Ratified May 7, 1992.*
No law, varying the compensation for the services of the Senators and Representatives, shall take effect, until an election of representatives shall have intervened.